False T[...]

Julia Donaldson

Illustrated by François Hall

Fairy Number 15 stood in a line with all the other new tooth fairies.

None of them had proper names because the Fairy Queen said that numbers were better.

The Fairy Queen gave each fairy two sacks and a map.

"The blue sack is for teeth and the red sack is for money," she said. "*Don't* mix them up. Now, have a look at your maps. The red crosses on them show where there are houses with children."

Fairy 15's map was of a town called Doddering. There weren't very many red crosses on it. She peeped at Fairy 14's map. It was of a town called Chattering. Chattering was near Doddering, and had lots and lots of red crosses.

"Off you fly!" said the Queen. "And remember, any fairy who is not back by six o'clock will lose her job."

Fairy 15 flew to Doddering. She tapped on a door with her magic wand.

Ping! she was inside.

Two boys were asleep in a bedroom. The fairy looked under both pillows. No teeth.

"Oh well, better luck next time," she said.

But she was wrong. There were no teeth under the pillows in the next house. Or the next one. Or the one after.

It seemed that none of the children in Doddering had lost any teeth.

The fairy was getting worried. What would the Fairy Queen say if she came back with no teeth at all in her sack?

Then she found a girl who was asleep with her mouth open. One of her teeth looked very wobbly.

"I'll just help it on its way," said the fairy. She took the tooth in both hands and started to wobble it. Yes! It was getting looser.

But just then the girl woke up. The fairy flew out of the room.

A loud snoring noise was coming from another bedroom. She crept in.

An old man lay asleep. On the table by his bed was a glass of water. And in the water was a set of teeth! The fairy counted the teeth. There were 32.

She fished them out with the old man's pipe, and put them into the blue sack. She tipped all the money out of the red sack.

Then she flew back to Fairyland.

The Fairy Queen was very pleased when she saw the set of teeth. But all she said was, "You can do better next time."

"Someone's hidden my teeth," said the old man when he woke up. "Was it you, Rachel?"

"No, Grandad," said the girl with the wobbly tooth.

The old man looked everywhere.
In the end he had to go and ask the dentist to make him some new ones.

That night, Fairy 15 brought back two sets of false teeth to Fairyland. The next night she brought back three sets. Then four. And so on.

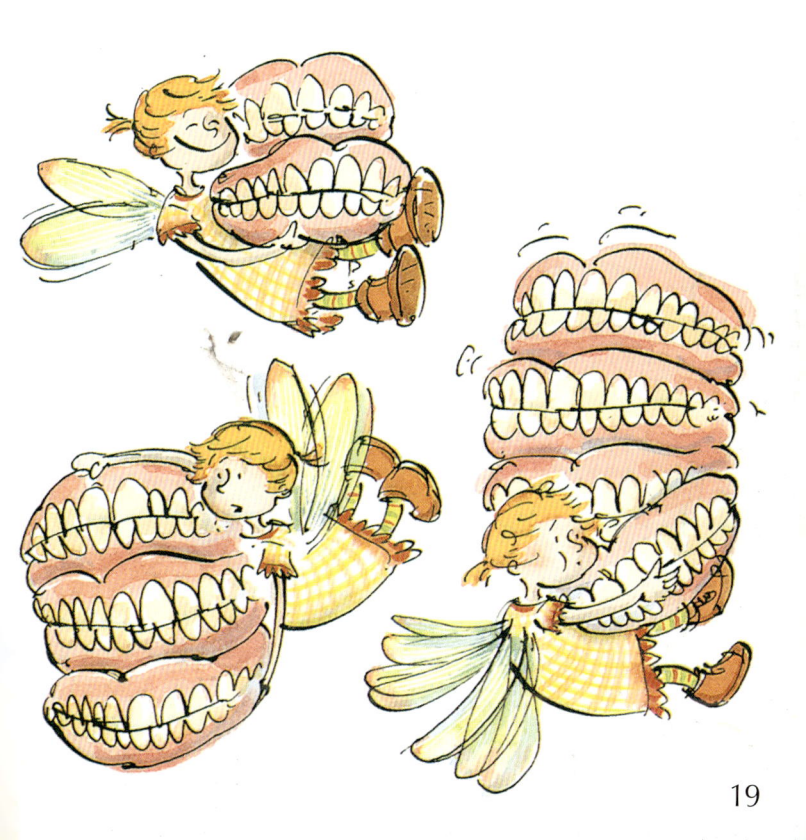

The Fairy Queen was very, very pleased, but all she ever said was, "You can do better next time."

The sack of teeth was growing heavier each night. The fairy's back started to ache, and she felt tired all the time. It wasn't much fun being a tooth fairy.

The dentist was feeling tired too.
He had never been so busy. He was
making new false teeth for all the
old people in Doddering.

One night, Fairy 15 tapped on a door with her wand. She didn't know that this was where the dentist worked.

When she saw his room she couldn't believe her eyes. There were false teeth everywhere! In no time at all the blue sack was full. But it was very heavy! And Fairy 15 was very tired.

"I'll just have a little rest," she said.

She lay down on the dentist's big chair. And that was where he found her the next morning.

Fairy 15 woke up.

"Help!" she said. "What's the time?"

"Nine o'clock," said the dentist.

"Oh no! I'm late!" said the fairy, and burst into tears.

"Have a hanky," said the dentist.

The fairy dried her eyes. Then she started crying again.

"The Fairy Queen will be so cross with me!" she said. "I'll lose my job."

The dentist gave her another hanky. He was a very kind man. Soon the fairy was telling him all about her job and her bad back.

"Are you sure you *want* to keep your job?" asked the dentist.

"No," said the fairy. "But what else can I do?"

"Well," said the dentist, "I could do with a tooth fairy. Would you like to work for me?"

"I'd *love* to," said the fairy.

"Good," said the dentist. "You can start today. My name's Mr White. What's yours?"

"I don't have a name," said the fairy sadly. "The Fairy Queen liked numbers better."

"We'll soon sort that out," said Mr White.

So now the tooth fairy is happy.
She gives badges to the children
from Doddering and Chattering. She
tells them how to look after their
teeth so that they will never need
false ones.

And sometimes she helps Mr White look in their mouths.

Her back is much better. And she has a badge of her own. It has her new name on it: "Ruth Mary, the Tooth Fairy".